8th Grade Common Core Math Workbook

Daily Practice Questions & Answers That Help Students Succeed

ISBN: 978-1-951806-28-6

FREE BONUS

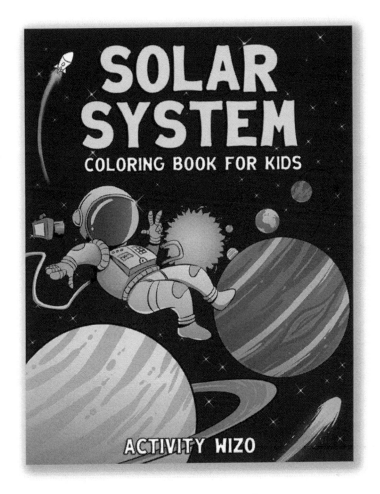

Get This FREE Bonus Now!

Just go to: activitywizo.com/free

Table of Contents

Section 1: The Number System

Rational Numbers and Irrational Numbers
By now, you should have learned that numbers can be classified in a variety of ways. The value of a number and how it is formed helps classify what type of number it is.

Mathematicians pay attention to the following types of numbers:

Whole numbers: Numbers that do not need to be represented as a fraction or decimal. These are also known as the counting numbers. Examples would be 4, 17, 29, 331.

Integers: All the whole numbers and their negative opposites. Examples would be -12, -6, 4, 13, 28.

Rational numbers: Numbers that can be expressed as a fraction of two integers. May be written as a fraction or as a decimal.
Whole numbers and integers are also rational numbers.
Examples would be 0.75, -12/18, $\sqrt{25}$

Irrational numbers: Numbers that cannot be expressed as a fraction of two integers. They number can only be expressed as an approximation as a decimal or with other symbols.
Examples would be 7π, $\sqrt{8}$

Let's practice.

Identify the numbers.
1. Is 22 rational or irrational? _____

2. Is $\sqrt{15}$ rational or irrational? _____

3. Is 14 rational or irrational? _____

4. Is π rational or irrational? _____

5. Is $\sqrt{49}$ rational or irrational? _____

6. Is $\sqrt{14}$ rational or irrational? _____

7. Is $\frac{4}{\pi}$ rational or irrational? _____

8. Is $\frac{31}{32}$ rational or irrational? _____

9. Is $\sqrt{164}$ rational or irrational? _____

10. Is $\frac{1}{3}$ rational or irrational? _____

11. Is $\sqrt{121}$ rational or irrational? _____

12. Is 6 rational or irrational? _____

13. Is $\sqrt{200}$ rational or irrational? _____

14. Is 11 rational or irrational? _____

15. Is $\frac{4}{6}$ rational or irrational? _____

16. Is 4π rational or irrational? _____

17. Which number is a whole number?
    a. $\sqrt{6}$
    b. $\frac{1}{6}$
    c. -6
    d. 6

18. Which number is a rational number?
    a. $\sqrt{5}$
    b. $\sqrt{8}$
    c. $\sqrt{9}$
    d. $\sqrt{10}$

19. Which number is an integer?
    a. -5
    b. -1.5
    c. $-\sqrt{5}$
    d. -5π

20. Which number is a rational number?
    a. $\frac{\pi}{3}$
    b. $3 + \pi$
    c. 3π
    d. $\sqrt{\pi}$

21. Which number is an irrational number?
    a. $\sqrt{4}$
    b. $\sqrt{10}$
    c. 4
    d. 10

22. Which number is an integer?
    a. -1.4
    b. 1.4
    c. -14
    d. $-\pi$

23. Which number is a rational number?
    a. $\sqrt{67}$
    b. $\sqrt{66}$
    c. $\sqrt{65}$
    d. $\sqrt{64}$

24. Which number is a whole number?
   a. -6
   b. 6
   c. $\frac{1}{6}$
   d. 6π

25. Which number is an integer?
   a. -102
   b. -1.02
   c. -10.2
   d. 100.2

26. Which number is an irrational number?
   a. $\frac{19}{20}$
   b. 19.19
   c. 19
   d. 19π

27. Which number is a whole number?
   a. -8.1
   b. $\sqrt{84}$
   c. 81
   d. -81

28. Which number is an irrational number?
   a. $\sqrt{61}$
   b. $\frac{1}{3}$
   c. $\frac{5}{6}$
   d. $\frac{\sqrt{61}}{5}$

29. Which number is an integer?
   a. $\sqrt{10}$
   b. -8.6
   c. 8.6
   d. -10

30. Which number is a whole number?
   a. -216
   b. 216
   c. $\frac{21}{6}$
   d. $-\sqrt{216}$

Converting Rational Numbers

Rational numbers can exist both in decimal and fraction form. You can use operations to convert numbers from decimal to fraction and also from fraction to decimal form.

Let's look at a few examples.

To convert a number from decimal to fraction form, you need to take the decimal and replace it over the hundreds place.
The number 0.225 can be converted to fraction form.
First, you see how far the decimal goes. In this case, the 5 is in the thousandths place.
You rewrite the number as a fraction 225/1000.
Then, you simplify the numerator and denominator.
Dividing both by 25 gives you 9/40.
So, the number 0.225 can be represented by the fraction $\frac{9}{40}$

To convert a number from fraction to decimal form, you divide the numerator by the denominator.
The number 7/20 can be converted to decimal form.
You divide 7 by 20 and solve the problem until you get a decimal that repeats or ends.
In this case, 7 divided by 20 gives you 0.35.
So, the number $\frac{7}{20}$ can be represented by the decimal 0.35

Let's practice!

Convert the decimals to their equivalent fractions.

31. 0.8125

32. 0.75

33. 0.375

34. 0.4

35. 0.62

36. 0.125

37. 0.27

38. 0.59375

39. 14.21

40. 36.15

41. 22.5

42. 6.625

43. 10.0625

44. 2.8

45.100.003

46. 11.72

Convert the fractions to their equivalent decimals.

47. 2/4

48. 4/5

49. 7/8

50. 8/10

51. 6/15

52. 5/16

53. 1/2

54. 5/100

55. 9 2/1000

56. 21 9/25

57. 19 3/4

58. 15 29/100

59. 6 101/500

60. 7 7/50

61. 32 1/5

62. 3 3/5

Approximate irrational numbers

When we look at irrational numbers, it is impossible to calculate their actual value.
We can approximate their value depending on the information we are given.

Let's look at an example.
When we are given an irrational number in terms of pi, we can calculate that value using the approximations of pi we have: $\frac{22}{7}$ or the decimal approximation of 3.14.
That means, when we are given a number of 4π, we can multiply 4 and pi and end up with an approximation of 12.56.

Let's look at another example.
Many times, we are given irrational numbers such as $\sqrt{24}$.
We can use our calculator to get an approximation or we can do it manually.
To do it manually, first you need to consider what perfect squares are near 25.
24 is between 16 and 25. The squares of those numbers are 4 and 5.
We know the square will be closer to 25 than 16 as 24 is closer to 25.
Let's start with 4.8. 4.8 squared is 23.04, 4.9 squared is 24.01
Let's get closer2 4.85 squared is 23.52, 4.88 squared is 23.814, 4.89 squared is 23.912
The approximate value of $\sqrt{24}$ is 23.912.

Let's practice!
Provide an approximate value for each irrational number given.

63. 8π 64. $\sqrt{32}$

65. $\sqrt{89}$ 66. $\sqrt{14}$

67. $\sqrt{60}$ 68. 10π

69. $\sqrt{6}$ 70. $\sqrt{115}$

71. 20π 72. $\sqrt{93}$

73. $\sqrt{50}$ 74. $\sqrt{28}$

Compare irrational numbers

We can compare irrational numbers to each other as well as to rational numbers.

When we compare numbers, we want to make sure they are in the same form.

First, convert both numbers to decimal or fraction form and then, compare.

Let's practice!

Convert both numbers to the same form and then fill in the appropriate sign: <, >, or =.

75. $\sqrt{28}$_____ $4\frac{5}{6}$

76. 10π _____ $\frac{32}{\pi}$

77. $\frac{1}{3}$ _____ $\frac{5}{12}$

78. $\sqrt{36}$ _____ 2π

79. 7.625 _____ $7\frac{12}{15}$

80. $11\frac{19}{32}$ _____ 11.59375

81. 5π _____ 15.8

82. $\sqrt{121}$ _____ 3π

83. 103.375 _____ $103 \frac{3}{8}$

84. $\sqrt{169}$ _____ 13

85. $\sqrt{16}$ _____ 5π

86. $\sqrt{28}$ _____ 5

87. $\frac{15}{16}$ _____ 0.78125

88. 9.3 _____ $\sqrt{88}$

89. 42.6875 _____ $42 \frac{11}{16}$

90. $\sqrt{62}$ _____ 7.5

Section 2: Operations with Numbers

Exponent Review

You have spent time in previous years working with exponents.
Remember, an exponent is composed of two numbers: the base and the power.

In the exponent x^2, x is the base and 2 is the power.

The base is the number or variable that is multiplied and the power is the number of times it is multiplied.

For x^2, you multiply the variable x twice. You can write it in expanded form by writing $x \cdot x$.

Let's practice!

Write each exponent below in expanded form.

91.　　4^5 　　　　　　　　　　　　　　　　92. 3^2

93.　　2^8 　　　　　　　　　　　　　　　　94. y^4

95.　　6^1 　　　　　　　　　　　　　　　　96. 5^3

97.　　a^2 　　　　　　　　　　　　　　　　98. 2^6

Negative Exponents

Do you remember how to handle a negative exponent? When you have a negative exponent, you should follow the negative exponent rule.

Negative Exponent Rule: $a^{-n} = \frac{1}{a^n}$

That means when you have a negative exponent, its value is the equal exponent value but its inverse.

Looking at real numbers: $7^{-2} = \frac{1}{7^2} = \frac{1}{49}$

Let's practice!

Simplify each negative exponent.

99. 4^{-2}

100. 2^{-8}

101. 3^{-1}

102. 8^{-4}

103. 5^{-5}

104. 9^{-3}

105. y^{-3}

106. n^{-4}

Combining Exponents

There are rules you can follow for combining exponents.

When you multiply two exponents with the same base, you add their powers.

When you divide two exponents with the same base, you subtract their powers.

Let's look at an example:

$$7^2 \times 7^4 = 7^{(2+4)} = 7^6$$

Let's practice!

107. $5^8 \div 5^2$

108. $3^5 \times 3^2$

109. $4^2 \times 4^{10}$

110. $8^9 \div 8^4$

111. $2^6 \div 2^3$

112. $5^2 \times 5^2$

113. $7^9 \div 7^2$

114. $7^2 \div 7^1$

115. $3^3 \times 3^4$

116. $4^6 \times 4^7$

117. $6^{10} \div 6^7$

118. $10^4 \div 10^3$

119. $2^1 \times 2^8$

120. $2^4 \times 2^4$

121. $9^{11} \div 9^6$

122. $6^3 \times 6^7$

Square roots

Now that we have reviewed exponents, let's take a look at some special cases, starting with squares.

When we take the square of a number, we multiply the number by itself. That is represented by the exponent: x^2, which we know means $x \cdot x$.

We can take what we know about squares and use it to find the square root of a number.

The square root of a number is the number that we multiply by itself to get the result. The symbol for square root is $\sqrt{}$.

For example, the square root of 16 is 4 because 4 times 4 equals 16. Mathematically, this looks like: $\sqrt{16} = 4$

Let's practice!
Find the square root of each number.

123. $\sqrt{121}$ 124. $\sqrt{4}$

125. $\sqrt{49}$ 126. $\sqrt{144}$

127. $\sqrt{36}$ 128. $\sqrt{64}$

129. $\sqrt{9}$ 130. $\sqrt{81}$

Cube roots

Similarly, when we take the cube of a number, we multiply the number by itself three times. That is represented by the exponent: x^3, which we know means $x \cdot x \cdot x$.

We can take what we know about cubes and use it to find the cube root of a number.

The cube root of a number is the number that we multiply by itself three times to get the result. The symbol for cube root is $\sqrt[3]{}$.

For example, the cube root of 125 is 5 because 5 times 5 times 5 equals 125.

Mathematically, this looks like $\sqrt[3]{125} = 5$

Let's practice!

Find the cube root of each number.

131. $\sqrt[3]{1000}$

132. $\sqrt[3]{512}$

133. $\sqrt[3]{216}$

134. $\sqrt[3]{8}$

135. $\sqrt[3]{27}$

136. $\sqrt[3]{729}$

137. $\sqrt[3]{64}$

138. $\sqrt[3]{343}$

What is scientific notation?

Have you ever had to read a very large number or small number.
When you start adding a lot of 0s, numbers can get hard to say.
We use scientific notation to express and do operations with large and small numbers easier.

How does it work?
When you use scientific notation, the number is broken into two parts.
The first part contains the actual digits of a number.
The second part contains the power that shows you how large or small the number is (how many zeros it should have).

Let's look at a few examples.
The number 9,620,000,000 can be expressed in scientific notation.
First, you rewrite the digits to a number that falls between 0 and 10.
So, 9,620,000,000, becomes 9.62
Then, you could the number of zeros you need to add to get to the large number.
Imagine in your head that 9,620,000,000 becomes 9.620000000
How many times do you need to move the decimal to the right to get the same number?
You should have counted 9 times.
So the number in scientific notation becomes 9.62×10^9.

Decimals work in a similar way.
Let's look at 0.00000000761
First, you rewrite the digits to a number that falls between 1 and 10.
So, 0.00000000761 becomes 7.61
Then, you could the number of zeros you need to add to get to the small number.
Imagine in your head that 0.00000000761 becomes 7.61
How many times do you need to move the decimal to the left to get the same number?
You should have counted 9 times.
So the number in scientific notation becomes 7.61×10^{-9}

Scientific notations with positive powers are large numbers with many zeroes.

Scientific notation with negative numbers are small numbers with many zeroes.

Let's practice!

Rewrite the number in scientific notation.

139. 2,890,000,000,000

140. 0.0000416

141. 1,500,000

142. 21,340,000,000

143. 0.00000081

144. 0.00427

145. 750,000,000,000

146. 0.00000000007

Rewrite the number in standard form.

147. 3.21×10^{-3}

148. 1.84×10^{13}

149. 8.74×10^5

150. 9.65×10^{-7}

151. 2.749×10^4

152. 7.318×10^{-11}

153. 4.964×10^{-6}

154. 5.555×10^8

Operations with Scientific Notation

Adding and subtracting numbers in scientific notation is quite simple, once you remember the numbers need to be to the same power.

We can use the distributive property to rearrange the powers so we are able to add the values.

Let's look at an example.

$$(2.78 \times 10^3) + (7.86 \times 10^5) =$$

We can rewrite (7.86×10^5) as $(7.86 \times 10^3 \times 10^2)$

We want the value to be 10^3 so we multiply the 10^2 to get rid of it.
$(7.86 \times 10^3 \times 10^2)$ becomes (786×10^3)
Now we can add $(2.78 \times 10^3) + 786$
First, we get 788.78×10^3. Now, we need to turn that number in scientific notation.
788.78×10^3 becomes 7.8878×10^5, which is our answer.

It works the same way with subtraction also.

Multiplication and division of numbers in scientific notation is easier, if we remember the exponent rule.
When we multiply two numbers in scientific notation, we multiply the coefficients and then add their exponents.
When we divide two numbers in scientific notation, we divide the coefficients and then subtract their exponents.

Let's practice!

155. $(2.31 \times 10^{-6}) + (5.87 \times 10^{-4})$

156. $(6.72 \times 10^{12}) \div (3.41 \times 10^{3})$

157. $(1.803 \times 10^{8}) \times (8.44 \times 10^{3})$

158. $(1.921 \times 10^{-8}) - (4.38 \times 10^{-6})$

159. $(7.64 \times 10^{-5}) \times (2.36 \times 10^{4})$

160. $(6.32 \times 10^{-8}) + (5.31 \times 10^{-5})$

161. $(9.63 \times 10^4) \div (6.41 \times 10^2)$

162. $(1.73 \times 10^8) - (7.62 \times 10^6)$

163. $(3.19 \times 10^{-8}) - (7.84 \times 10^{-7})$

164. $(4.39 \times 10^{15}) \div (2.37 \times 10^5)$

165. $(9.43 \times 10^4) \times (2.64 \times 10^3)$

166. $(1.83 \times 10^{14}) + (2.79 \times 10^{16})$

Section 3: Expressions and Equations

Graphing Proportional Relationships
When we look at how two values interact, when they change based on each other, we describe them as being a relationship.
We describe the relationship as being proportional if one value increases as the other increases. We can show this as a graph.
Check out the graph below.
It shows the relationship y=3x.

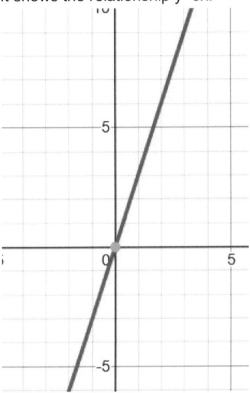

What this means is to calculate, the y value, you multiply the x value by 3.
Each value of x is directly proportional to each y value by 3.
Let's practice calculating coordinate values so we can graph.
For each problem, give the y coordinate using the x value and the rate of proportionality.

167. y=2x   x=3   168. y=20x   x=2

169. y=10x x=1   170. y=4x   x=5

171. y=6x   x=4   172. y=12x   x=6

173. y=3x   x=10   174. y=8x   x=9

Unit Rate and Slope

When we look at the graph, the proportional value can also be known as the unit rate or slope. The slope of the line is defined as its rate of change from one value to the next.

You can find the slope of any line using two of its points.

To find the slope, you should use the following formula.

Slope (m)= $\frac{y_2-y_1}{x_2-x_1}$

Let's look at an example.

The line passes through the points (8, 3) and (4, 1). What is its slope? Use the formula!

$$\frac{y_2 - y_1}{x_2 - x_1} = \frac{3 - 1}{8 - 4} = \frac{2}{4} = \frac{1}{2}$$

So based on the formula, every point on this line is one unit above and two units to the right of the point before it.

Let's practice!

Use the slope formula to find the slope of two points.

175.   (2, 10) and (-1, 2)   176. (0, -7) and (36, 2)

177.   (-4, 0) and (5, 18)   178. (6, 6) and (15, 9)

179.   (3, 15) and (1, 5)   180. (12, 0) and (30, 3)

181. (4, 15) and (-2, -3)   181. (2, 20) and (4, 40)

Slope-Intercept Form

When we graph lines, we one way we graph the line is by using slope-intercept form.

When a line is in slope-intercept form, it follows a specific format. Slope-intercept is always written as $y = mx + b$, where m is the slope of the line and b is the y-intercept.

You can rewrite equations given in other ways, into slope intercept form to allow you to easily graph the line.

Let's practice.

Identify the slope.

183. $y = 4x + 7$

184. $y = \frac{1}{8}x + 5$

185. $y = -2x - 4$

186. $y = -\frac{2}{3}x + 6$

187. $y = -10x - 8$

188. $y = \frac{3}{5}x - 4$

189. $y = 14x + 14$

190. $y = -3x + 20$

Identify the y-intercept.

191. $y = -2x - 22$

192. $y = \frac{1}{3}x + 15$

193. $y = -6x - 13$

194. $y = 10x - 25$

195. $y = \frac{3}{4}x + 14$

196. $y = 0.6x + 2.75$

197. $y = -\frac{8}{9}x + 45$

198. $y = -4x + 12$

Rewrite in slope-intercept form.

199. $3y - 12x = 6$

200. $5y = x + 10$

201. $4y + 2x = 28$

202. $4x - 196 = 14y$

203. $3y + 33 = 42x$

204. $\frac{1}{3}y - 2 = x$

205. $5x - 3 = \frac{1}{2}y$

206. $8y - 1 = 3x$

Linear Equations

Do you remember how to solve linear equations?

When solving equations for an unknown variable, you should work in REVERSE order of operations and attempt to get the variable on its own. Also, everything you do to one side of the equation, you should do to the other.

Let's work through an example:

$$12x + 2 = 38$$

First, we need to subtract 2 from both sides.
$$12x + 2 - 2 = 38 - 2$$

$$12x = 36$$

Divide both sides by 12.
$$12x \div 12 = 36 \div 12$$

You get the solution of $x = 3$.

Let's practice!

207. $-2x + 7 = 11$

208. $12x + 2 = 52$

209. $6x + 8 = 44$

210. $-3x - 7 = -10$

211. $-12x - 6 = 54$

212. $6x + 9 = 51$

213. $-8x + 11 = 15$

214. $5x + 10 = 55$

215. $7x - 17 = -17$

216. $-11x + 7 = -125$

217. $13x - 11 = -115$

218. $15x + 5 = -10$

219. $-7x + 7 = 35$

220. $-8x - 13 = -11$

221. $10x - 9 = 101$

222. $13x - 1 = 38$

223. $4x + 20 = 4$

224. $9x - 11 = -8$

225. $-6x - 10\ = 8$

226. $3x + 18 = 33$

227. $-10x + 6 = 86$

228. $7x + 4 = 18$

229. $8x + 10 = 90$

230. $-10x - 12 = -16$

Solve Pairs of Linear Equations

You can apply your knowledge of solving equations to solve two pairs of equations with two variables. If you are given equations with 2 variables and you have 2 equations, you can solve them to find each variable. Let's review how.

First, if you have 2 equations, the solution for both equations will be the coordinate where they overlap. This is true because it is the one spot on both equations where both x and y values are true.

You can also solve the equations algebraically.

Let's look at one way to do so-the substitution method.

Let's say you have the equations: $2x + 4y = 10$ and $x - y = 2$

You can solve one of the equations for a variable, x or y, and then substitute it into the other equation.

$2x + 4y = 10$ and $x - y = 2$

$x - y = 2$ becomes $x = y + 2$

Then, you substitute that equation into the first equation:

$2x + 4y = 10$ becomes $2(y + 2) + 4y = 10$

Then, you solve for y.

$$2y + 4 + 4y = 10$$
$$6y + 4 = 10$$
$$6y = 6$$
$$y = 1$$

Then, you substitute y into the original equation to find x.

$x - y = 2$ becomes $x - 1 = 2$

Add 1 to both sides.

$$x = 3$$

So the solution for the set of equations is (3, 1).

Let's practice! Solve each set of equations.

231. $2x + 3y = 10$

$y = \frac{1}{2}x + 1$

232. $x + 5y = -2$

$y = \frac{2}{7}x + 3$

233. $y = 3x - 4$

$2x + 3y = 32$

234. $5x + 2y = 9$

$3x + 2y = -1$

235. $y = -\frac{1}{3}x - 4$

$\quad\;\; y = -\frac{1}{2}x - 5$

236. $6x + 2y = -1$

$\quad\;\;\; y = 8x - 6$

237. $10x = 30y = 15$

$\quad\;\; 2x + 3y = 21$

238. $14x + 7y = 34$

$\quad\;\; 10x + 3y = 31$

239. $y = 12x + 2$

$\quad\;\; y = \frac{1}{3}x + 19.5$

240. $2x - 3y = 5$

$\quad\; -4x - 3y = -55$

Section 4: Functions

What is a function?

A function is a special type of relationship in math.

In math, when we are talking about functions, we are talking about a relationship that connects an input to an output.

Let's look at a simple example:

Multiply by 4 is a function.

Review the table below to see how the function works.

Input	Relationship	Output
1	× 4	4
2	× 4	8
3	× 4	12

When we write functions as relationships, we write them as f(x)= 4x.

This means the function of x is defined as x times 4.

The x, takes the place of the input and shows us how to calculate the output.

Let's practice!

241. For the function $f(x) = x + 4$, define the output if the input equals 9?

242. For the function $f(x) = 2x$, define the input if the output equals 80?

243. For the function $f(x) = x^2$, define the input if the output equals 16?

244. For the function $f(x) = 8x - 3$, define the output if the input equals 2?

245. For the function $f(x) = 10x + 2$, define the output if the input equals 4?

246. For the function $f(x) = \frac{1}{2}x - 5$, define the input if the output equals 1?

247. For the function $f(x) = 12x - 5$, define the output if the input equals 7?

248. For the function $f(x) = 6x + 11$, define the input if the output equals 29?

The Graph of a function

We graph functions just like we graph equations! We can graph a function by defining a few x values (inputs) and then using them to calculate the outputs. Then, we can connect the points and draw our lines.
Let's look at an example:

$$f(x) = \frac{1}{3}x + 4$$

$f(3) = 5$
$f(6) = 6$
$f(9) = 7$

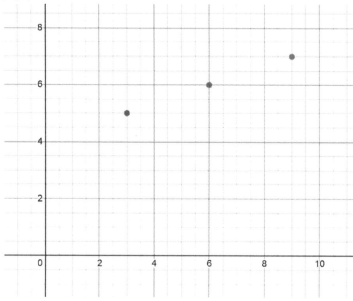

Then, connect the points.

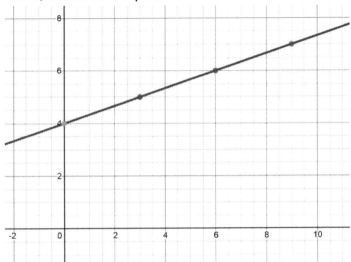

Let's practice!

Graph the following functions.

249. $f(x) = 4x$

250. $f(x) = -5x - 3$

251. $f(x) = \frac{3}{7}x + 2$

252. $f(x) = \frac{-x}{3}$

Representing functions

We can represent functions in different ways. There are three main ways you will see a function represented. A function can be represented as a(n)

- Equation
- Graph
- Table

When a function is represented as an equation, it usually uses the f(x) format we talked about earlier.

An example of a function as an equation would be f(x)= 4x.

The same function can be represented as a graph:

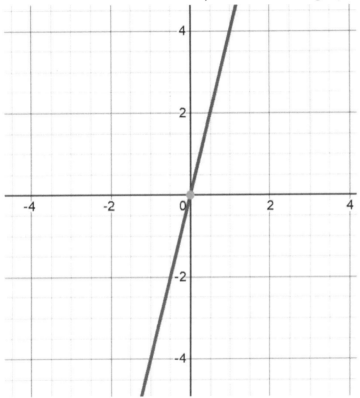

It can also be represented as a table:

x	y
-2	-8
3	12
12	48

All three representations show the same function.
We can use the different representations of a function to help us solve different types of problems.

Let's practice!
How would you represent each given function as a graph?

253. $f(x) = \frac{3}{4}x - 1$

254. $f(x) = x^2 + 3$

255. $f(x) = 5x$

266. $f(x) = \frac{2}{7}x + 4$

257. $f(x) = x^3$

258. $f(x) = 8x$

259. $f(x) = -\frac{1}{2}x - 6$

260. $f(x) = -3x$

How would you represent each given function as an equation?

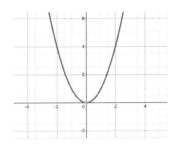

261.

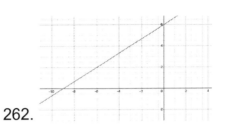

262.

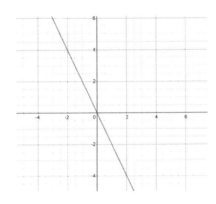

263.

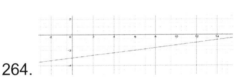

264.

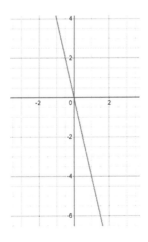

265.

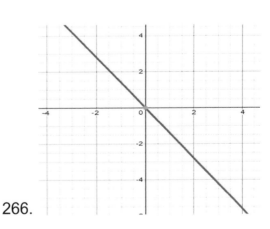

266.

267.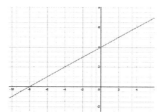

268.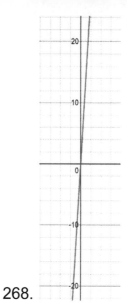

What would be the missing value in each table?

269. $f(x) = 6x$

x	y
-1	-6
0	0
4	?

270. $f(x) = \frac{1}{5}x - 4$

x	y
-5	-5
0	-4
10	?

271. $f(x) = x^2 + 2$

x	y
-2	6
0	2
3	?

272. $f(x) = -\frac{2}{3}x + 6$

x	y
-6	10
-3	8
3	?

273. $f(x) = -9x$

x	y
-4	36
0	0
10	?

274. $f(x) = -7x$

x	y
-6	42
1	-7
5	?

275. $f(x) = \frac{2}{9}x - 10$

x	y
-9	-12
0	-10
18	?

276.

x	y
-3	15
1	-5
2	?

Linear functions and Non-Linear Functions

Have you noticed some of the graphs we looked at were straight lines and some were not? Remember, the definition of a function is a relationship where each input has a single output.

A function DOES not have to be a straight line!

For example:

x	y
-2	7
4	12
4	10

This would not be a function because the input 4 gives you 2 different output values.

We can also use a vertical line to test the function of a graph.
If a vertical line goes through two points of the tested function, it is not defined as a function.

Here is an example of a graphed line that is not a function:

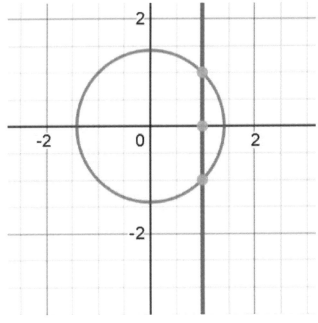

Functions can be defined as linear and non-linear.

A linear function is a function whose graph is a line. Linear functions also have a constant rate of change, or slope.

If a function is not a straight line, it is defined as a nonlinear function.

Let's practice!
Is the line a function?

277.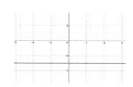

278.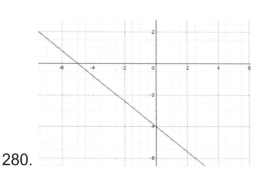

279.

280.

281. The line contains the points (3, 3), (-2, 5) and (3, -3)

282. The line contains the points (-12, 4), (6, 11) (14, 11)

283. The line contains the points (-6, 4) (-5, 10), (2, 22)

284. The line contains the points (-4, -2), (-7, -2), (6, -2)

Is the function linear or non-linear?

285.

286.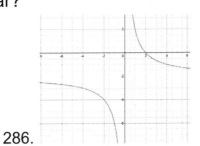

287.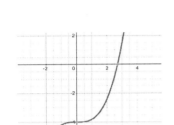

288.

289.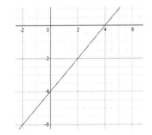

290.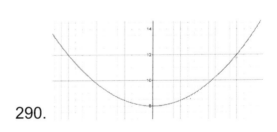

Comparing functions

Looking at linear and non-linear functions, one way to help analyze a function is by looking closer at its slope or rate of change.
Linear functions have a constant slope. Non-linear functions have a slope that changes.

Functions can also be increasing and decreasing.
When a function is increasing, as the x values increase, so do the y values.
When a function is decreasing, as the x values increase, the y values decrease.

You can use information about the slope and whether a function is increasing or decreasing to compare functions.

Let's practice!
Circle the function that has a larger rate of change.

291. $y = \frac{2}{3}x + 6$

OR

0	9
1	12
2	15

292. $y = 4x + 7$

OR

$$y = x + 4$$

293.

3	1
6	2
9	3

OR

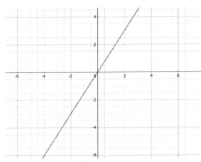

294. $y = -\frac{3}{2}x - 10$

OR

-2	-4
-1	-2
0	0

295. $y = 5x$

OR

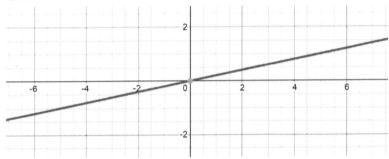

Circle the function that has a smaller rate of change.

296.

5	40
7	56
9	72

OR

$$y = 10x - 1$$

297.

1	-1
2	-4
3	-9

OR

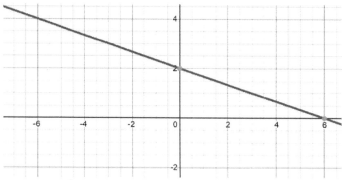

298. $y = \frac{1}{5}x - 2$

OR

5	3
10	6
15	9

299. $y = -\frac{1}{3}x + 4$

OR

1	6
2	12
3	18

300. $y = 14x$

OR

$$y = -14x + 7$$

Let's practice all we learned about equations and functions and solve some word problems!

301. Write an equation for the following situation.
Marissa bought some t-shirts. Each shirt cost $26. She also paid a tax of 5% on her purchase. If she spent $163.80, how many shirts did she buy?

302. Solve the equation for the solution to the problem above.

303. Solve the problem below.
The sum of three consecutive numbers is 51. What are the 3 numbers?

304. Evelyn has $12 to spend on school supplies. If pencils cost $0.60 and pens cost $1.20, and she wants at least 8 pens, how many pencils can she buy?

305. You are taking a test worth 100 points that contains 60 questions. There are true false questions worth 1 point and vocabulary questions worth 2 points. How many of each type of question are on the test?

Section 5: Geometry

Changing Shapes

When we look at shapes in geometry, there are ways we move shapes that changes the way the shape appears, but keeps the shape the same size.

There are 4 major ways we move shapes:

- Rotation: when we rotate a shape, we turn it around a central point.
- Translation: when we translate a shape, we move it to a different place.
- Reflection: when we reflect a shape, we flip the shape along a line called the mirror line.

Let's look at an example.

Here is our original shape.

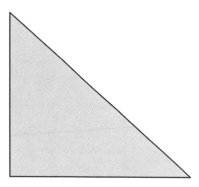

If we were to rotate it, it would look like this:

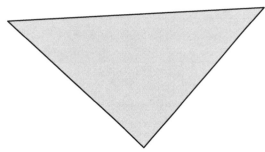

To translate it on the coordinate plane, it would stay the same shape and appearance but move an appropriate number of units.

To reflect it, it would look like this:

We can also change the size of a shape through dilation.

When we dilate a shape, we keep the angle size the same, but we make it larger or smaller based on a proportion.

Let's look at an example.

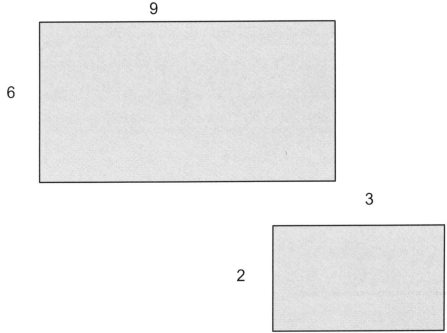

This rectangle was reduced by 3. To do this, we divided the original rectangle

Let's practice!
Look at the shape drawn. Rotate or reflect a shape based on directions given and draw the new shape.
306. Rotate

307. Reflect

308. Reflect

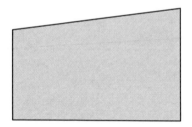

309. Rotate

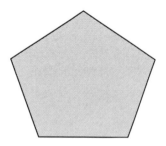

310. Rotate

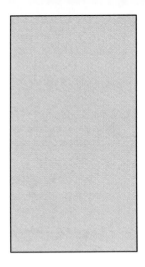

311. Reflect

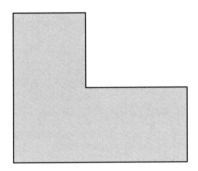

312. Rotate

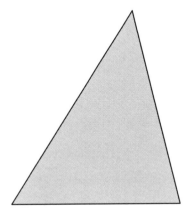

313. Rotate

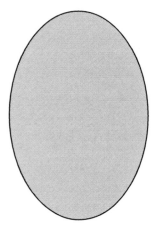

Look at the shape drawn and the measurements provided. Dilate the shape and provide the new measurements based on the proportion given.

314. Dilate twice as large.

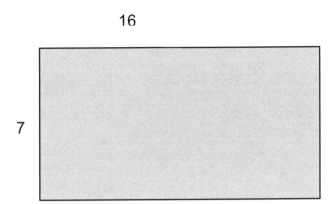

315. Dilate by ⅕

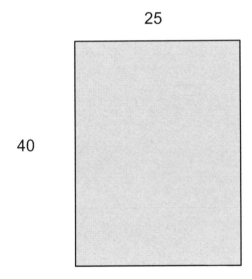

316. Dilate by ¼

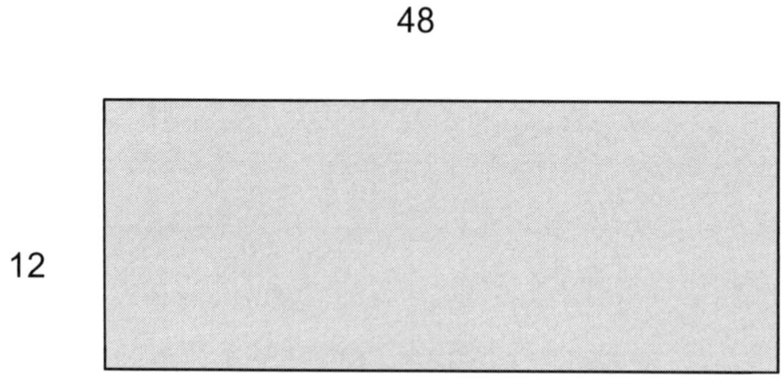

48

12

317. Dilate six times as large.

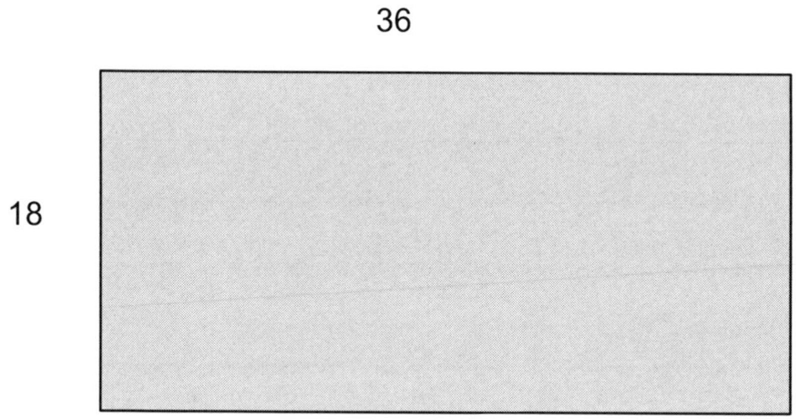

36

18

318. Dilate by ½

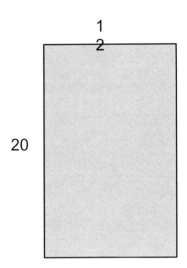

1
2

20

319. Dilate three times as large.

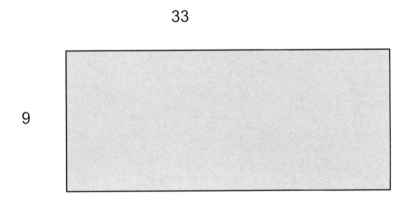

33

9

320. Dilate four times as large.

24

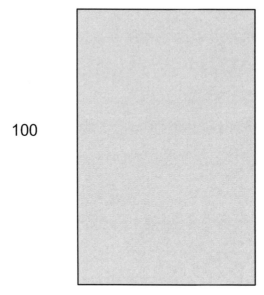

100

Comparing Shapes

When we look at shapes and compare them to others, two ways we can describe shapes are as similar or congruent.

Two shapes are similar if they have the same properties but are different sizes. To get similar shapes, we need to rotate, reflect or translate one shape and then dilate it.

Here are similar shapes.

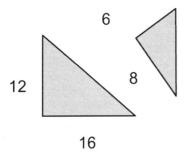

Two shapes are congruent if they have the same properties but are the same size. To get a congruent shape, we only rotate, reflect or translate a shape.

Here are congruent shapes.

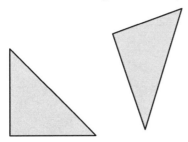

Let's practice!
Circle the similar shapes.
321.

322.

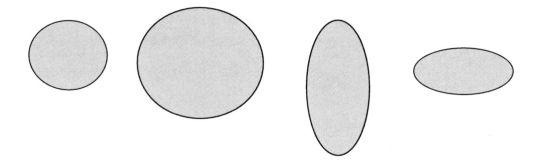

323.

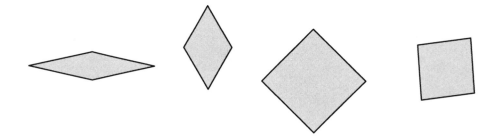

324.

Circle the congruent shapes.

325.

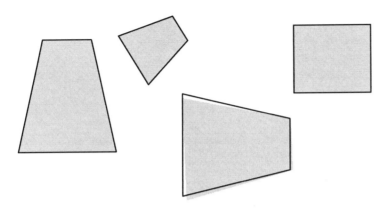

326.

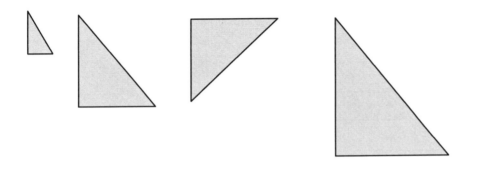

327.

Parallel lines

In geometry, we examine parallel lines in relationship to each other and other lines to make meaning of angle measurements.

Review the image below:

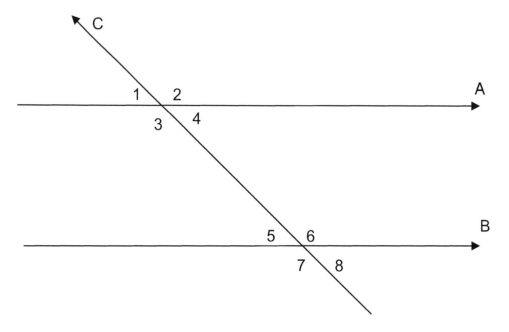

When the parallel lines are cut by another parallel line, this is called "a parallel line cut by a transversal." We can define the relationship between some of the angles as follows:

Lines 1 and 4, 2 and 3, 5 and 8 and 6 and 7 are all vertical angles. Each pair of vertical angles has the same measurement.
We also know that each adjacent angle pair is equal to 180°, so each adjacent angle pair is also supplementary.
We also have sets of special angles that are equal:
Corresponding angles: 1 and 5, 2 and 6, 3 and 7, 4 and 8
Alternate exterior angles: 1 and 8, 2 and 7
Alternate interior angles: 3 and 6, 4 and 5

We can use what we know about angle congruence and supplementary angles to provide angle measurements when given other measurements.

Let's practice!

Use the information provided about parallel lines to find the missing angle measurements:

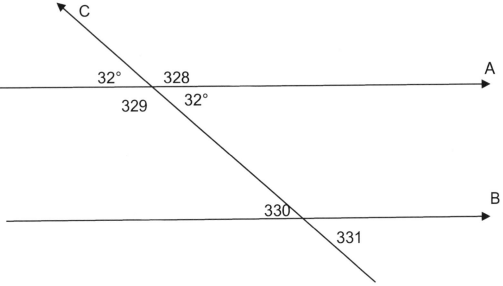

328.

329.

330.

331.

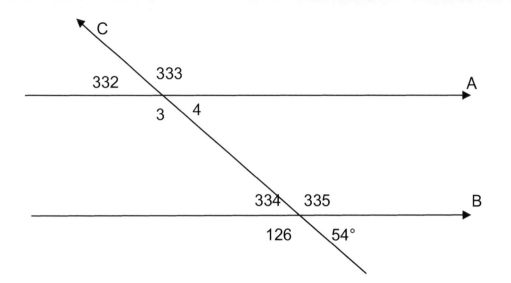

332.

333.

334.

335.

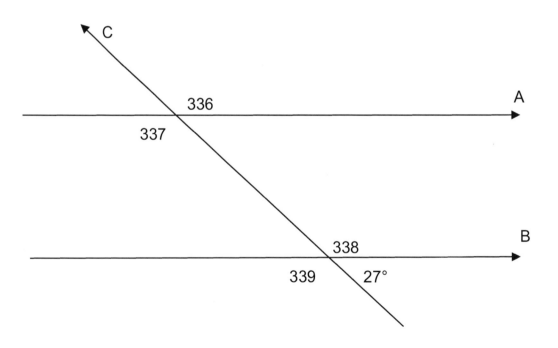

336.

337.

338.

339.

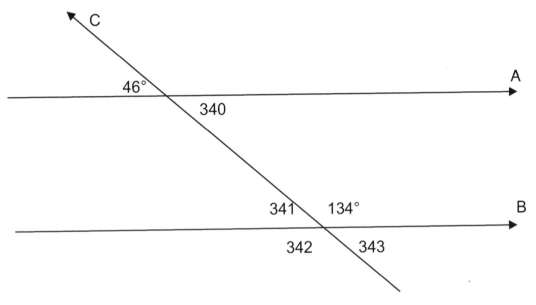

340.

341.

342.

343.

The Pythagorean Theorem

You should have learned about the Pythagorean Theorem last year. That is the formula: $a^2 + b^2 = c^2$, where a and b are the sides of a right triangle and c is the longest side or hypotenuse. But did you know it began by looking at squares?

When a triangle has one right angle, and you make a square on each side, the largest square's area is equal to the area of the other 2 squares!

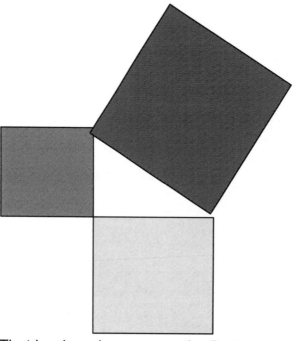

That is why, when we use the Pythagorean Theorem we square the sides because the area of the triangles is equal NOT the length of the sides.

We can use the Pythagorean Theorem to find the measurement of an unknown side in a right triangle.

Let's look at an example.
You are given 2 lengths of a right triangle: 5 and 12. What is the measurement of the hypotenuse or c?

$$a^2 + b^2 = c^2$$
$$5^2 + 12^2 = c^2$$
$$25 + 144 = c^2$$
$$169 = c^2$$
$$13 = c$$

Let's practice!

344. One side of a right triangle is 7 and the hypotenuse is 25. What is the length of the second side?

345. Two sides of a right triangle are 11 and 60. What is the measurement of the hypotenuse?

346. One side of a right triangle is 3 and the hypotenuse is 5. What is the length of the second side?

347. Two sides of a right triangle are 20 and 21. What is the measurement of the hypotenuse?

348. Two sides of a right triangle are 8 and 15. What is the measurement of the hypotenuse?

349. One side of a right triangle is 6 and the hypotenuse is 10. What is the length of the second side?

350. Two sides of a right triangle are 12 and 16. What is the measurement of the hypotenuse?

351. One side of a right triangle is 10 and the hypotenuse is 26. What is the length of the second side?

Volume of cones, cylinders and spheres
Have you noticed that cylinders and cones are similarly shaped?
If a cylinder and cone share the same radius and height, a cone can fit within a cylinder.
Actually, a cone is ⅓ the size of a cylinder.

If the volume of a cylinder is $V = \pi r^2 h$, then the volume of the cone is $V = \frac{1}{3}\pi r^2 h$.

If a cylinder's radius is twice as large as a sphere's, the sphere will fit inside a cylinder.

This impacts the volume of a sphere. The volume of a sphere is $V = \frac{4}{3}\pi r^3$.

You can use these formulas to calculate the volume of these solids.
Let's practice!

352. Cylinder, r=5, h=10   353. Sphere, r=6

354. Cone, r=7, h=13   355. Cylinder, r=10, h=2

356. Sphere, r=4   357. Cone, r=1, h=4
358. Cylinder, r=3, h=8   359. Sphere, r=11

Section 6: Statistics and Probability

Surveying and Random Samples
Have you ever taken a part in a survey?

If you have, you have been part of data gathering for one study or another. When we collect data in a survey, we ask people questions and record their answers. We then use that information to draw conclusions about larger groups of people.

Let's look at an example:

Amelia surveyed 80 students at her school about their favorite subject. Of those surveyed, 20 chose science as their favorite subject. If there are 600 students in the whole school, around how many like science?

      a. 200
      b. 80
      c. 300
      d. 150

If Amelia got 20/80 students to choose science, that means about 25% of the student body likes science best. She can apply that analysis to the whole student body to determine how many students out of 600 like science.

25% of 600 is _____. To solve, you take 25% or 0.25 multiplied by 600. When you do so, you get an answer of 150 students like science.

When we look at collecting information, we want to do so in a random sample. This means we want to ask people's whose opinions or conditions reflect the variety of people who can be found in the larger population about whom we are trying to draw conclusions.

When we analyze data, we want to be sure the information we gather is accurate.

Let's look at an example:

Alex is trying to construct a random sample to make inferences about how many students have siblings. If the total population is 300, which amount would be an acceptable random sample?

    a. 3
    b. 13
    c. 45
    d. 200

We want our random sample to be small enough to be a manageable amount but to be large enough to allow us to draw some conclusions about the data. In this case, c, or 45 is really the best number to base our data on.

Let's practice!

360. You want to figure out if students will recycle after lunch in your school. What would be the best group to use as a random sample?

    a. 20 teachers
    b. Administrators
    c. 20 random people
    d. 20 random students in the lunchroom

361. You want to know which cartoon is most popular with 8 year olds. What would be the best random sample?

    a. 50 10 year olds
    b. 50 8 year olds
    c. 50 6 year olds
    d. 50 kids of random ages

362. From 2000 cars produced, the manufacturer took a random sample of 50 cars. Of those 50, 2 had a defect. Estimate the total number of defective cars.

    a. 65
    b. 80
    c. 105
    d. 405

363. From 7500 TVs produced, the manufacturer took a random sample of 30 TVs. Of those 30, 1 had a defect. Estimate the total number of defective TVs.

a. 200
b. 250
c. 300
d. 250

364. You want to know how popular basketball is at your school. Which group would give you the best random sample?
      a. A selection of students from mandatory gym class
      b. A selection of the tallest students
      c. A selection of the smallest students
      d. A selection of students from the basketball team

365. You want to know which restaurant in your town is most popular. Which group would give you the best random sample?
      a. A selection of people at the local mall
      b. A selection of people at an expensive restaurant
      c. A selection of teens in your neighborhood
      d. A selection of elderly people from your church

366. You want to know how many elementary students bring their lunch to school. Which group would give you the best random sample?
      a. 30 1st graders
      b. 30 6th graders
      c. 30 10th graders
      d. 30 elementary parents

367. You want to know how many students have chores to do at home. Which group would give you the best random sample?
      a. 4 students in your grade
      b. 40 students in your grade
      c. 400 students in your grade
      d. 4000 students from your town

368. You want to know how many kids like to go to the beach on vacation. Which group would give you the best random sample?
      a. 20 kids at a park
      b. 20 kids on the beach
      c. 20 kids from your school
      d. 20 kids hiking in the woods

369. You want to know what students' favorite sport is. Which group would give you the best random sample?

       a. A group of students on your baseball team
       b. A group of students who run track
       c. A group of students from your gym class
       d. A group of students who go to all the football games

370. You want to know how students spend their summer break. Which group would give you the best random sample?

       a. 1 kid from the hallway
       b. 5 kids from the hallway
       c. 10 kids from the hallway
       d. 50 kids from the hallway

Drawing Conclusions from Data

371. According to the results of last year's standardized tests, 20% of 6th graders scored above grade level in math. What is a valid conclusion to make?

    a. If there are 100 6th grade students, 40 are above grade level.

    b. If there are 400 6th grade students, 40 are above grade level.

    c. If there are 200 6th grade students, 40 are above grade level.

    d. If there are 300 6th grade students, 40 are above grade level.

372. According to the results of last year's standardized tests, 40% of 8th graders scored below grade level in math. What is a valid conclusion to make?

    a. If there are 150 8th grade students, 120 are below grade level.

    b. If there are 150 8th grade students, 60 are below grade level.

    c. If there are 150 8th grade students, 80 are below grade level.

    d. If there are 150 8th grade students, 80 are below grade level.

373. According to the results of last year's standardized tests, 30% of 7th graders scored on grade level in math. What is a valid conclusion to make?

    a. If there are 200 students, 60 are above grade level.

    b. If there are 200 students, 60 are below grade level.

    c. If there are 200 students, 90 are on grade level.

    d. If there are 200 students, 60 are on grade level.

374. A company wants to add a new flavor of ice cream. They conduct sample tests with three flavors. The data showed 65% liked mango, 20% liked dragonfruit and 10% did not like either. What is a valid conclusion to make?

       a. Mango is the flavor the company should add.
       b. Dragonfruit is the flavor the company should add.
       c. The company should do more research.
       d. The company should not add either flavor.

375. A company wants to add a new flavor of ice cream. They conduct sample tests with three flavors. No clear flavor had a majority of people who enjoyed it. What is a valid conclusion to make?

       a. The company should do more research.
       b. The company should add all three flavors.
       c. The company should try three other flavors.
       d. The company should pick one flavor to add.

Probability

Have you played a game where you roll the dice and try to figure out your chances of getting a certain number. Your chances of doing something are called the probability of an event.

To calculate the chances of something happening, you can create a sample space.

To do this, you lay out all possibilities of an event occurring.

Let's look at an example:

Create a sample space to show the possibilities of rolling a die, twice and getting 2 5s.

1-1	2-1	3-1	4-1	5-1
6-1				
1-2	2-2	3-2	4-2	5-2
6-2				
1-3	2-3	3-3	4-3	5-3
6-3				
1-4	2-4	3-4	4-4	5-4
6-4				
1-5	2-5	3-5	4-5	5-5
6-5				
1-6	2-6	3-6	4-6	5-6
6-6				

376. You toss three coins. Show your sample space of possibilities.

377. You choose a shirt and a pair of pants from the following color choices:

Shirt: blue, green, gray, purple, white; Pants: blue, khaki, black
Show your sample space of possibilities.

To calculate the probability of an event, you consider the likelihood of the event you want over the likelihood of all possible events.

Let's look at an example:
What is the probability you will flip a coin and get a heads?

The chance of getting a heads is 1 (you can either get a heads or tails) and the total outcomes you can achieve is 2 (a heads or tails). That makes the probability ½. You express probability as a fraction, which you should reduce if you can.

Let's practice!

378. You toss three coins. Find P (3 heads)
  a. ⅛
  b. 1/9
  c. ⅓
  d. 6/9

379. You toss three coins. Find P (two tails)
  a. 2/3
  b. 3/4
  c. 4/5
  d. 5/6

380. You have 2 number cubes. Find P(1 and 6)
  a. 1/36
  b. 2/18
  c. 4/18
  d. 2/9

381. You have 2 number cubes. Find P(2 and 2)
 a. ⅙
 b. 1/10
 c. 1/24
 d. 1/36

382. You have 2 number cubes. Find P(3 and 4)
 a. 4/36
 b. 3/36
 c. 1/36
 d. 2/36

383. You have 2 number cubes. Find P(sum of cubes is 12)
 a. 1/36
 b. 2/36
 c. 3/36
 d. 4/36

You choose a shirt and a pair of pants from the following color choices:
 Shirt: blue, green, gray, purple, white; Pants: blue, khaki, black

384. You choose a shirt and a pair of pants. P(same color shirt and pants)
 a. ⅕
 b. ¼
 c. ⅓
 d. 1/15

385. You choose a shirt and a pair of pants. P(khaki pants)
 a. ⅕
 b. ⅓
 c. ¼
 d. 1/15

386. You choose a shirt and a pair of pants. P(green shirt)
       a. ⅕
       b. ⅓
       c. ½
       d. 1/6

When looking at probability of more than one event, you should consider whether the outcomes of the first event impacts the following events.

If events are independent, you calculate the probability of each event as it comes.
For dependent events, be sure to consider the events that happen when considering the outcomes.

Identify the probability of the events being independent or dependent.

387._____ Drawing a king from a deck of cards, then another king

388. _____ Flipping a coin twice in a row

389. _____ You roll a die 3 times in a row.

390. _____ You take a marble out of a bag and then grab 3 more marbles.

391. You roll a number twice. What is the probability that you will roll a 3, then an even number?
       a. 12/36
       b. 9/36
       c. 6/36
       d. 3/36

392. You roll a number twice. What is the probability that you will roll an odd number, then an even number?

    a. 9/36
    b. 7/36
    c. 5/36
    d. 3/36

You have 15 socks: 4 blue socks, 6 black socks and 5 white socks. Find the probability you will pick

393. A white sock

    a. ⅓
    b. ⅕
    c. 1/7
    d. 1/15

394. A blue sock

    a. 1/15
    b. 2/15
    c. 3/15
    d. 4/15

395. A black sock

    a. 2/15
    b. 3/15
    c. 4/15
    d. 6/15

396. Two white socks

    a. 2/15
    b. 5/7
    c. 4/15
    d. 6/15

Section 7: Review Problems

Tell whether the given number is rational or irrational.

397. 5π

398. 4.2893646237863482876

399. $\frac{2}{3}$

400. $\sqrt{12}$

Circle the integers in each set.

401. 6, -4, 3.8, -1.5, 16, -20

402. $-\frac{5}{8}, \sqrt{16}, -7, 21, 0.875$

Circle the whole numbers in each set.

403. 13, 0.65, -2, 11, 7.6, -1.3

404. $-6, -4, -1, -\frac{4}{5}, -0.75, -\frac{8}{3}$

Convert the given decimals to fractions.

405. 0.36

406. 3.2575

Convert the given fractions to decimals.

407. $14\frac{79}{90}$

Approximate the square root to the nearest tenth.

408. $\sqrt{87}$

Circle the larger number.

409. $\sqrt{17}$ or 4.5

410. 10π or 30

Circle the smaller number.

411. 2π or $\sqrt{52}$

412. $\sqrt{81}$ or 3π

Rewrite the exponent in expanded form.

413. 4^5

414. 2^7

415. 12^3

416. 3^0

Simplify the given negative exponent.

417. 2^{-3}

418. 8^{-2}

419. $\dfrac{6}{3^{-4}}$

420. $4(2^{-3})$

Combine the exponents.

421. $2^3 + 2^8$

422. $11^4 - 11^0$

Write the given numbers in scientific notation.

423. 4,612,000,000,000

424. 0.00000027381

425. 0.00000000009372

426. 8,027,500,000,000

427. 6,017,000,000

428. 0.00000000005021

Write the given numbers in standard form.

429. 1.419×10^8

430. 6.10182×10^{-12}

431. 9.126×10^4

432. 8.2513×10^{-10}

433. 5.412×10^{-7}

434. 7.1296×10^6

Solve the given problems (operations in scientific notation).

435. $(5.716 \times 10^{-7}) + (2.1274 \times 10^{-7})$

436. $(3.729 \times 10^{-6}) \times (4.21 \times 10^3)$

437. $(3.124 \times 10^{-8}) - (1.642 \times 10^{-8})$

438. $(3.127 \times 10^{-4}) \div (2.61 \times 10^{-2})$

439. $(2.124 \times 10^5) \times (8.5 \times 10^5)$

440. $(2.6193 \times 10^4) + (1.8273 \times 10^6)$

441. $(9.236 \times 10^{10}) - (6.127 \times 10^9)$

442. $(9.315 \times 10^{12}) \div (3.16 \times 10^6)$

For each problem, give the y coordinate using the x value and the equation provided.

443. $y = x^3, x = 9$

444. $y = 4x - 7, x = 2$

445. $y = \frac{1}{4}x + 3, x = 12$

446. $y = 8x, x = 0$

Provide the slope of the line with the information provided.

447. (3, -2) and (18, 8)

448. $y = 5x - 7$

Identify the y-intercept of the line with the information provided.

449. $y = \frac{4}{5}x + 20$

450. $y = 6x - 12$

Rewrite the line provided in slope-intercept form.

451. $2x + 4y = 12$

452. $-15x + 5y = 10$

453. $20y + 20 = 4x$

454. $24x - 4y = 28$

Solve each equation provided for the unknown variable.

455. $x + 7 = 14$

456. $2x - 4 = 8$

457. $x + 6 = 20$

458. $4x - 5 = 7$

459. $-3x - 2 = 4$

460. $10 - x = 2$

461. $-10x - 8 = 12$

462. $9x - 18 = -18$

Solve each system of equations.

463. $y = 6x + 2, y = 4x + 4$

464. $y = -\frac{1}{3}x + 6, y = 3x - 34$

465. $y = 5x + 4, y = 7x$

466. $y = 2x - 10, y = 4x - 16$

467. $y = \frac{2}{5}x - 7, y = \frac{2}{10}x - 5$

468. $y = 3x - 7, y = -2x + 18$

469. $y = \frac{2}{7}x - 4, y = -\frac{1}{3}x + 9$

470. $y = 6x, y = 2x - 4$

471. For the function $f(x) = \frac{1}{2}x + 2$, define the input if the output equals 9?

472. For the function $f(x) = x^2$, define the output if the input equals 4?

473. Circle the similar shapes.

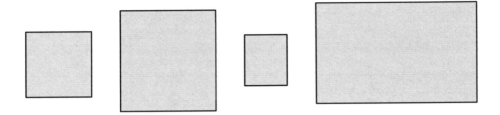

474. Circle the similar shapes.

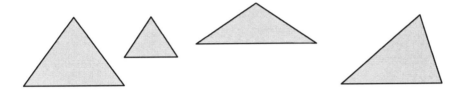

475. Circle the congruent shapes.

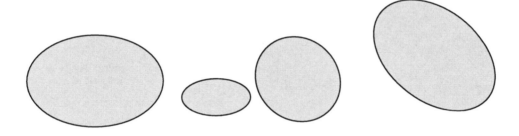

476. Circle the congruent shapes.

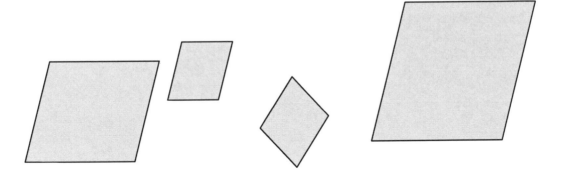

Use the information provided about parallel lines to find the missing angle measurements.

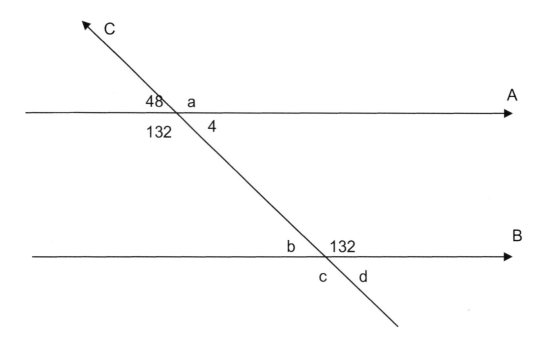

477.   a=?

478. b=?

479.   c=?

480. d=?

Use the Pythagorean Theorem to find the missing measurement.

481. Two sides of a right triangle are 12 and 16. What is the measurement of the hypotenuse?

482. Two sides of a right triangle are 24 and 32. What is the measurement of the hypotenuse?

483. One side of a right triangle is 28 and the hypotenuse is 53. What is the length of the second side?

484. Two sides of a right triangle are 15 and 36. What is the measurement of the hypotenuse?

485. One side of a right triangle is 16 and the hypotenuse is 65. What is the length of the second side?

486. One side of a right triangle is 40 and the hypotenuse is 50. What is the length of the second side?

Find the volume of the solid, using the measurements given.

487.   Cylinder, r=2, h=7

488. Cone, r=5, h=4

489.   Cylinder, r=6, h=1

490. Sphere, r=3

491. You want to know which music group is most popular with teenagers. What would be the best random sample?

    a. A group of teenagers at the mall
    b. A group of teenagers in the orchestra
    c. A group of families at the park
    d. A group of kids taken from first grade

492. You want to know which food is most popular for families for breakfast. What would be the best random sample?

    a. A group of students eating in the cafeteria
    b. A group of families grocery shopping
    c. A group of teachers cooking lunch
    d. A group of women at the park

493. From 10,000 buttons produced, the manufacturer took a random sample of 300. Of those 300, 230 were red. Estimate the total number of red buttons.

494. From 500 bicycles manufactured, the manufacturer took a random sample of 20 bikes. Of those 20, 2 had defects. Estimate the total number of defective bikes.

495. According to the results of last year's standardized tests, 15% of 8th graders scored below grade level in math. If there are 640 8th graders, how many scored on or above grade level?

496. According to the results of last year's standardized tests, 60% of 8th graders scored at grade level in math. If there are 800 8th graders, how many scored on grade level?

497. You choose a cookie and an ice cream flavor from the following choices:

Cookie: chocolate chip, sugar, peanut butter; Ice cream: chocolate, vanilla, strawberry, coffee

Show your sample space of possibilities.

498. You have a deck of cards. Find P(queen)

499. You have 1 number cube. Find P(not 4)

500. You have 2 number cubes. Find P(above 3)

Answers

Section 1
Rational Numbers and Irrational numbers
1. Rational
2. Irrational
3. Rational
4. Irrational
5. Rational
6. Irrational
7. Rational
8. Rational
9. Irrational
10. Rational
11. Rational
12. Rational
13. Irrational
14. Rational
15. Rational
16. Irrational
17. D
18. C
19. A
20. A
21. B
22. C
23. D
24. B
25. A
26. D
27. C
28. A
29. D
30. B

Converting rational numbers to decimal form
31. 13/16
32. ¾
33. ⅜
34. ⅖
35. 31/50

36. ⅛
37. 27/100
38. 19/32
39. 14 21/100
40. 36 3/20
41. 22 ½
42. 6 ⅝
43. 10 1/16
44. 2 ⅘
45. 100 3/1000
46. 11 18/25
47. 0.5
48. 0.8
49. 0.875
50. 0.8
51. 0.4
52. 0.3125
53. 0.5
54. 0.05
55. 9.002
56. 21.36
57. 19.75
58. 15.29
59. 6.202
60. 7.14
61. 32.2
62. 3.6

Approximate irrational numbers

63. 25.133
64. 5.657
65. 9.434
66. 3.742
67. 7.746
68. 31.416
69. 2.449
70. 10.724
71. 62.832
72. 9.644
73. 7.071

74. 5.292

Compare irrational numbers

75. >
76. >
77. <
78. <
79. <
80. =
81. <
82. >
83. =
84. =
85. <
86. >
87. >
88. <
89. =
90. >

Section 2 Answers

Exponent Review

91. $4 \cdot 4 \cdot 4 \cdot 4 \cdot 4$
92. $3 \cdot 3$
93. $2 \cdot 2 \cdot 2 \cdot 2 \cdot 2 \cdot 2 \cdot 2 \cdot 2$
94. $y \cdot y \cdot y \cdot y$
95. 6
96. $5 \cdot 5 \cdot 5$
97. $a \cdot a$
98. $2 \cdot 2 \cdot 2 \cdot 2 \cdot 2 \cdot 2$

Negative Exponents

99. $\frac{1}{4^2}$
100. $\frac{1}{2^8}$
101. $\frac{1}{3}$
102. $\frac{1}{8^4}$
103. $\frac{1}{5^5}$
104. $\frac{1}{9^3}$

105. $\dfrac{1}{y^3}$

106. $\dfrac{1}{n^4}$

Combining Exponents

107. 5^6
108. 3^7
109. 4^{12}
110. 8^5
111. 2^3
112. 5^7
113. 7^7
114. 7^1
115. 3^7
116. 4^{13}
117. 6^3
118. 10^1
119. 2^9
120. 2^6
121. 9^5
122. 6^{10}

Square Roots

123. 11
124. 2
125. 7
126. 12
127. 6
128. 8
129. 3
130. 9

Cube Roots

131. 10
132. 8
133. 6
134. 2
135. 3
136. 9
137. 4
138. 7

What is scientific notation?

139.	2.89×10^{12}
140.	4.16×10^{-5}
141.	1.5×10^6
142.	2.134×10^{10}
143.	8.1×10^{-7}
144.	4.27×10^{-3}
145.	7.5×10^{11}
146.	7×10^{-11}
147.	0.00321
148.	1,840,000,000,000
149.	87,400
150.	0.000000965
151.	27,490
152.	0.00000000007318
153.	0.000004964
154.	555,500,000

Operations with Scientific Notation

155.	5.8932×10^{-4}
156.	1.9707×10^9
157.	1.5217×10^{12}
158.	4.3608×10^{-6}
159.	1.803
160.	5.316×10^{-5}
161.	1.5023×10^2
162.	1.6538×10^8
163.	-7.521×10^{-7}
164.	1.852×10^{10}
165.	2.4895×10^8
166.	2.8083×10^{16}

Section 4: Expressions and Equations
Graphing Proportional Relationships

167.   6
168.   40
169.   10
170.   20
171.   24
172.   72
173.   30
174.   72

Unit Rate and Slope

175.   2.66
176.   ¼
177.   2
178.   ⅓
179.   5
180.   ⅙
181.   3
182.   10

Slope-Intercept Form

183.   4
184.   ⅛
185.   -2
186.   -⅔
187.   -10
188.   ⅗
189.   14
190.   -3
191.   (0, -22)
192.   (0, 15)
193.   (0, -13)
194.   (0, -25)
195.   (0, 14)
196.   (0, 2.75)
197.   (0, 45)
198.   (0, 12)
199. $y = 4x + 2$
200. $y = \frac{1}{5}x + 2$

201. $y = -\frac{1}{2}x + 7$

202. $y = \frac{2}{7}x - 14$

203. $y = 14x - 11$

204. $y = 3x + 6$

205. $y = 10x - 6$

206. $y = \frac{3}{8}x + \frac{1}{8}$

Linear Equations

207. x=-2
208. x=4.1667
209. x=6
210. x=1
211. x=-5
212. x=7
213. x=-1/2
214. x=9
215. x=0
216. x=12
217. x=-8
218. x=-1
219. x=-4
220. x=-1/4
221. x=11
222. x=3
223. x=-4
224. x=1/3
225. x=-3
226. x=5
227. x=-8
228. x=2
229. x=10
230. x=2/5

Solve Pairs of Linear Equations

231. (2, 2)
232. (-7, 1)
233. (4, 8)
234. (5, -8)
235. (-6, -2)
236. (0.5, -2)

237.	(7.5, 2)
238.	(4, -3)
239.	(1.5, 20)
240.	(10, 5)

Section 4: Functions

What is a function?

241.	13
242.	40
243.	4
244.	13
245.	42
246.	12
247.	79
248.	3

The Graph of a function

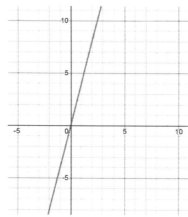

249.

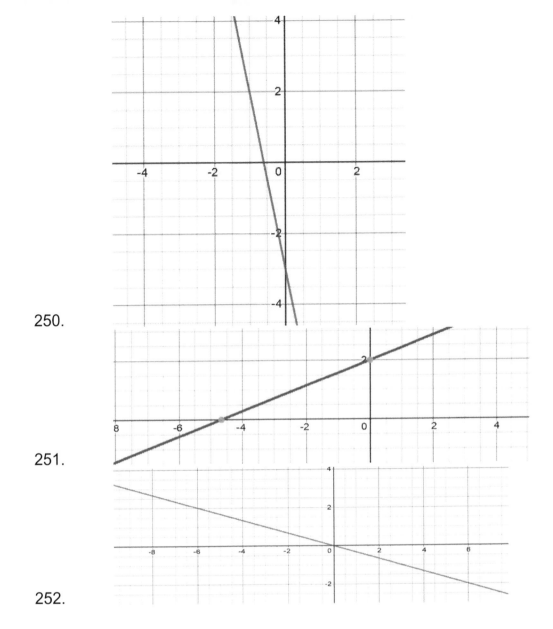

250.

251.

252.

Representing functions

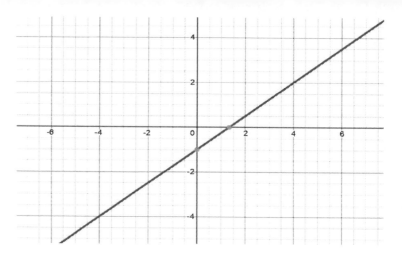

253.

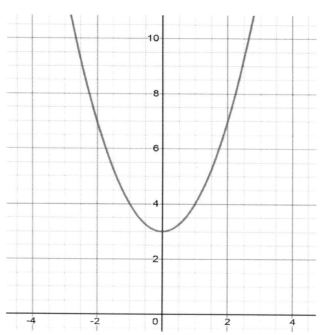

254.

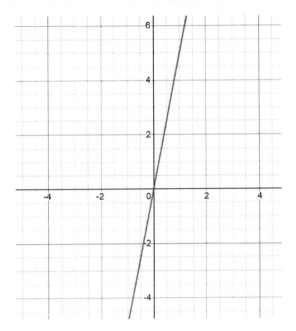

255.

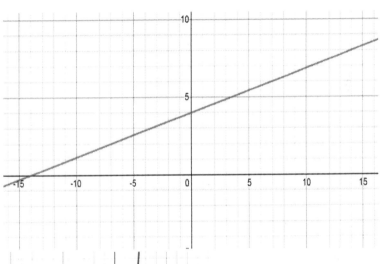

256.

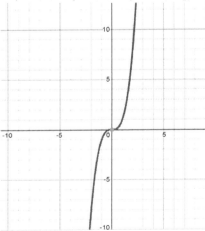

257.

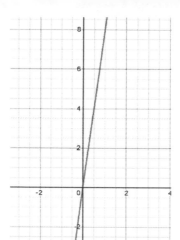

258.

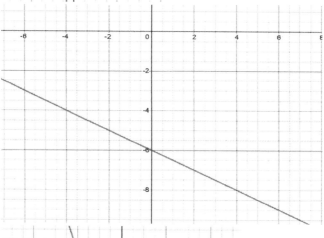

259.

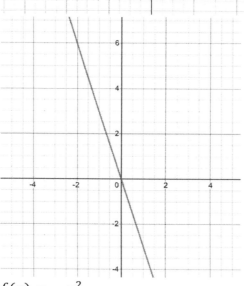

260.

261. $f(x) = -x^2$

262. $f(x) = \frac{2}{3}x + 6$

263. $f(x) = -2x$

264. $f(x) = \frac{1}{6}x - 3$

265. $f(x) = -4x$

266.	$f(x) = -\frac{7}{5}x$
267.	$f(x) = \frac{1}{2}x + 4$
268.	$f(x) = 14x$
269.	24
270.	-2
271.	11
272.	4
273.	-90
274.	-35
275.	-6
276.	-10

Comparing functions

277.	Yes
278.	No
279.	Yes
280.	Yes
281.	No
282.	No
283.	Yes
284.	Yes
285.	Linear
286.	Non-linear
287.	Non-linear
288.	Linear
289.	Linear
290.	Non-linear

Comparing functions

291.	Students should circle the table.
292.	Students should circle $y = 4x + 7$
293.	Students should circle the graph
294.	Students should circle the table
295.	Students should circle $y = 5x$
296.	Students should circle the table
297.	Students should circle the table
298.	Students should circle $y = \frac{1}{5}x - 2$
299.	Students should circle $y = -\frac{1}{3}x + 4$

300.   Students should circle $y = -14x + 7$

Word Problems
    301.   163.80= 0.05 (26x)+26x
    302.   x=6 shirts
    303.   16, 17, 18
    304.   4 pencils
    305.   20 true false, 40 vocabulary

Section 5: Geometry
Changing Shapes
    306.   Students should draw a shape that is similar in size but rotated around a point.
    307.   Students should draw a shape that is reflected over an imaginary line.
    308.   Students should draw a shape that is reflected over an imaginary line.
    309.   Students should draw a shape that is similar in size but rotated around a point.
    310.   Students should draw a shape that is similar in size but rotated around a point.
    311.   Students should draw a shape that is reflected over an imaginary line.
    312.   Students should draw a shape that is similar in size but rotated around a point.
    313.   Students should draw a shape that is similar in size but rotated around a point.
    314.   Students should draw a rectangle that is 32 long and 14 wide.
    315.   Students should draw a rectangle that is 5 long and 8 wide.
    316.   Students should draw a rectangle that is 12 long and 3 wide.
    317.   Students should draw a rectangle that is 216 long and 108 wide.
    318.   Students should draw a rectangle that is 6 long and 10 wide.
    319.   Students should draw a rectangle that is 99 long and 27 wide.

320.   Students should draw a rectangle that is 96 long and 400 wide.

Comparing Shapes
321.   Students should circle first and third shape.
322.   Students should circle first and second shape.
323.   Students should circle third and fourth shape.
324.   Students should circle second and third shape.
325.   Students should circle first and third shape.
326.   Students should circle second and third shape.
327.   Students should circle first and fourth shape.

Parallel lines
328.   148°
329.   148°
330.   32°
331.   32°
332.   54°
333.   126°
334.   54°
335.   126°
336.   153°
337.   153°
338.   153°
339.   153°
340.   46°
341.   46°
342.   134°
343.   46°

The Pythagorean Theorem
344.   24
345.   61
346.   4
347.   29
348.   17
349.   8
350.   20
351.   24

Volume of cones, cylinders and spheres
352.   785.4
353.   904.78

354.	660.39
355.	628.32
356.	268.08
357.	4.19
358.	226.19
359.	5575.28

Section 6: Statistics and Probability

Surveying and Random Samples

360.	D
361.	B
362.	B
363.	B
364.	A
365.	A
366.	D
367.	B
368.	C
369.	C
370.	D

Drawing Conclusions from Data

371.	C
372.	B
373.	D
374.	A
375.	A

Probability

376.	Students should create a line-up of all the possibilities.
377.	Students should create a line-up of all the possibilities.
378.	A
379.	A
380.	A
381.	D
382.	C
383.	A
384.	D
385.	B

386.	A
387.	Dependent
388.	Independent
389.	Independent
390.	Dependent
391.	C
392.	A
393.	A
394.	D
395.	D
396.	A

Section 7: Review Problems

397.	Irrational
398.	Rational
399.	Rational
400.	Irrational
401.	Students should circle 6, -4, 16 and -20.
402.	Students should circle 21.
403.	Students should circle 13 and 11.
404.	Students should not circle any numbers.
405.	$\frac{9}{25}$
406.	$3\frac{103}{400}$
407.	14.8$\underline{7}$
408.	9.3
409.	4.5
410.	10π
411.	2π
412.	$\sqrt{81}$
413.	$4 \times 4 \times 4 \times 4 \times 4$
414.	$2 \times 2 \times 2 \times 2 \times 2 \times 2 \times 2$
415.	$12 \times 12 \times 12$
416.	1
417.	$\frac{1}{8}$
418.	$\frac{1}{64}$
419.	$\frac{2}{27}$
420.	$\frac{1}{2}$

421.	2^{11}
422.	11^{-4}
423.	4.612×10^{12}
424.	2.7381×10^{-7}
425.	9.372×10^{-11}
426.	8.0275×10^{12}
427.	6.017×10^9
428.	5.021×10^{-11}
429.	141,900,000
430.	0.00000000000610182
431.	91,260
432.	0.00000000082513
433.	0.0000005412
434.	7,129,600
435.	7.8434×10^{-7}
436.	1.5699×10^{-2}
437.	1.482×10^{-8}
438.	1.198×10^{-2}
439.	1.8054×10^{11}
440.	1.8535×10^6
441.	8.6233×10^{10}
442.	2.9478×10^6
443.	y=729
444.	y=1
445.	y=6
446.	y=0
447.	$\frac{2}{3}$
448.	5
449.	(0, 20)
450.	(0, -12)
451.	$y = \frac{1}{2}x + 3$
452.	$y = 3x + 2$
453.	$y = \frac{1}{5}x - 1$
454.	$y = 6x - 7$
455.	x=7
456.	x=6
457.	x=14

458.	x=3
459.	x=-2
460.	x=8
461.	x=-2
462.	x=0
463.	(1, 8)
464.	(12, 2)
465.	(2, 14)
466.	(3, -4)
467.	(20, -1)
468.	(5,8)
469.	(21,2)
470.	(-1, -6)
471.	x=14
472.	16
473.	Students should circle the first three shapes.
474.	Students should circle the first two shapes.
475.	Students should circle the first and last shapes.
476.	Students should circle the second and third shapes.
477.	132
478.	48
479.	132
480.	48
481.	20
482.	40
483.	45
484.	39
485.	63
486.	30
487.	87.96
488.	104.72
489.	113.1
490.	113.1
491.	A
492.	B
493.	7667
494.	50 bicycles
495.	544
496.	480

497. Students should create a diagram of all different possible combinations.

498. 1/13

499. $\frac{5}{6}$

500. $\frac{1}{4}$

Made in the USA
Columbia, SC
07 June 2023

17812412R00070